W9-CKG-876

My First Animal Library

Bullfrogs

by Martha E. H. Rustad

Ideas for Parents and Teachers

Bullfrog Books let children practice reading informational texts at the earliest reading levels. Repetition, familiar words, and photo labels support early readers.

Before Reading

- Discuss the cover photo. What does it tell them?
- Look at the picture glossary together. Read and discuss the words.

Read the Book

- "Walk" through the book and look at the photos. Let the child ask questions. Point out the photo labels.
- Read the book to the child, or have him or her read independently.

After Reading

- Prompt the child to think more. Ask: Have you ever seen a bullfrog? Where was it? Did you hear it croak?

Bullfrog Books are published by Jump!
5357 Penn Avenue South
Minneapolis, MN 55419
www.jumplibrary.com

Library of Congress Cataloging-in-Publication Data
Rustad, Martha E. H. (Martha Elizabeth Hillman), 1975-
Bullfrogs / by Martha E.H. Rustad.
p. cm. -- (Bullfrog books. My first animal library, nocturnal animals)
Summary: "This easy-to-read nonfiction story tells a "night in the life" of a bullfrog, from waking up, finding food and finding a mate, to going back to sleep when the sun comes up"—Provided by publisher.
Audience: K to grade 3.
Includes bibliographical references and index.
ISBN 978-1-62031-073-1 (hardcover)
ISBN 978-1-62496-073-4 (ebook)
1. Bullfrog--Juvenile literature. I. Title.
QL668.E27R87 2014
597.8'92--dc23
2013004606

Editor Rebecca Glaser
Series Designer Ellen Huber
Book Designer Lindaanne Donohoe
Book Production Sean Melom

Photo Credits: All photos by Shutterstock except: Getty, 9; iStock, 8; National Geographic, 23bl, 23tl; SuperStock, 23br

Printed in the United States of America at Corporate Graphics in North Mankato, Minnesota.
4-2013 / PO 1003
10 9 8 7 6 5 4 3 2 1

Table of Contents

Bullfrogs at Night

The sun sets.
Night begins.
Bullfrogs wake up.

Bullfrogs hunt at night.
They watch and listen.
They look for bugs, fish, or mice.

A hungry bullfrog leaps.
Its big mouth grabs food.

Gulp!

webbed
feet

The bullfrog swims in the pond.

Water keeps its smooth skin wet.

Its webbed feet push through water.

The bullfrog hides.

A bird looks closely.

But it cannot see the hidden bullfrog.

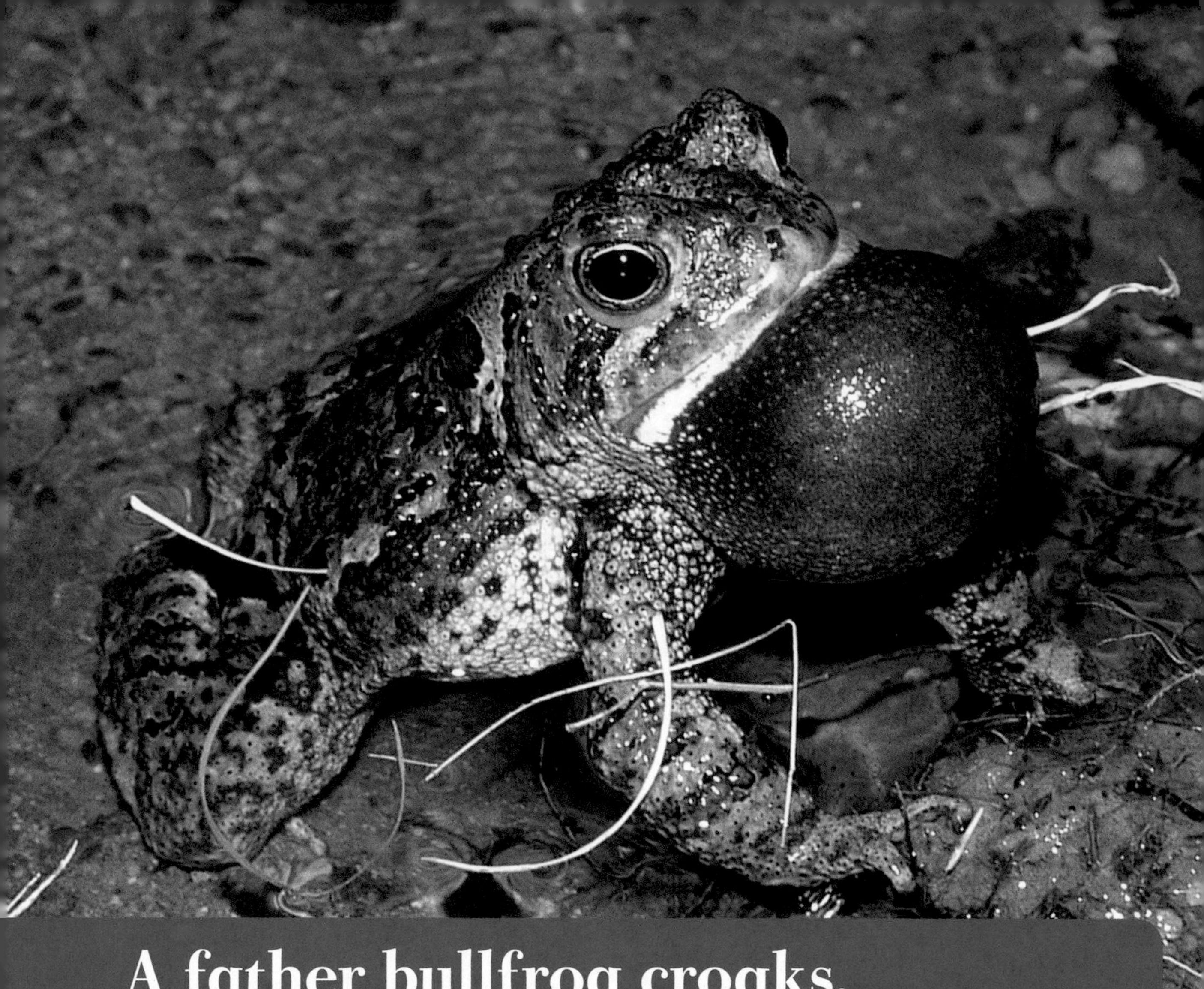

A father bullfrog croaks.
Croaks warn other male bullfrogs.

Fathers wrestle for the best ponds.

A mother listens for his croaks.

She lays many eggs in his pond.

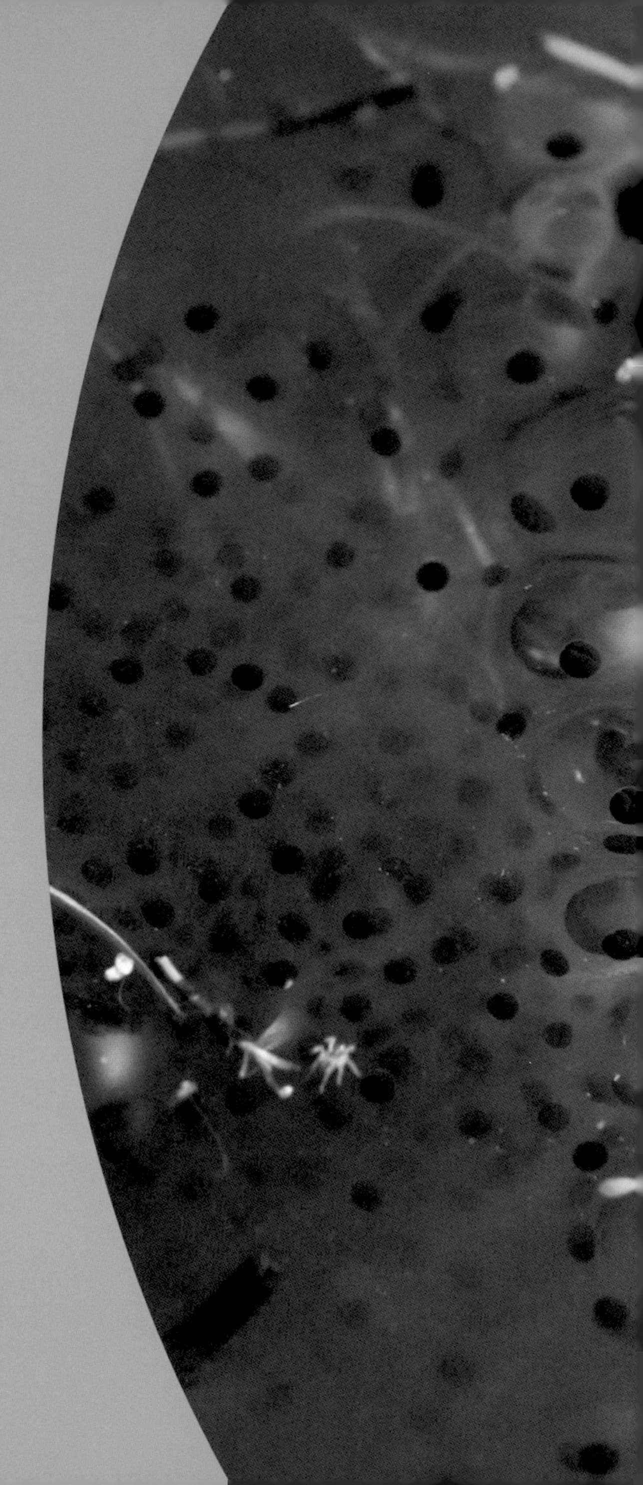

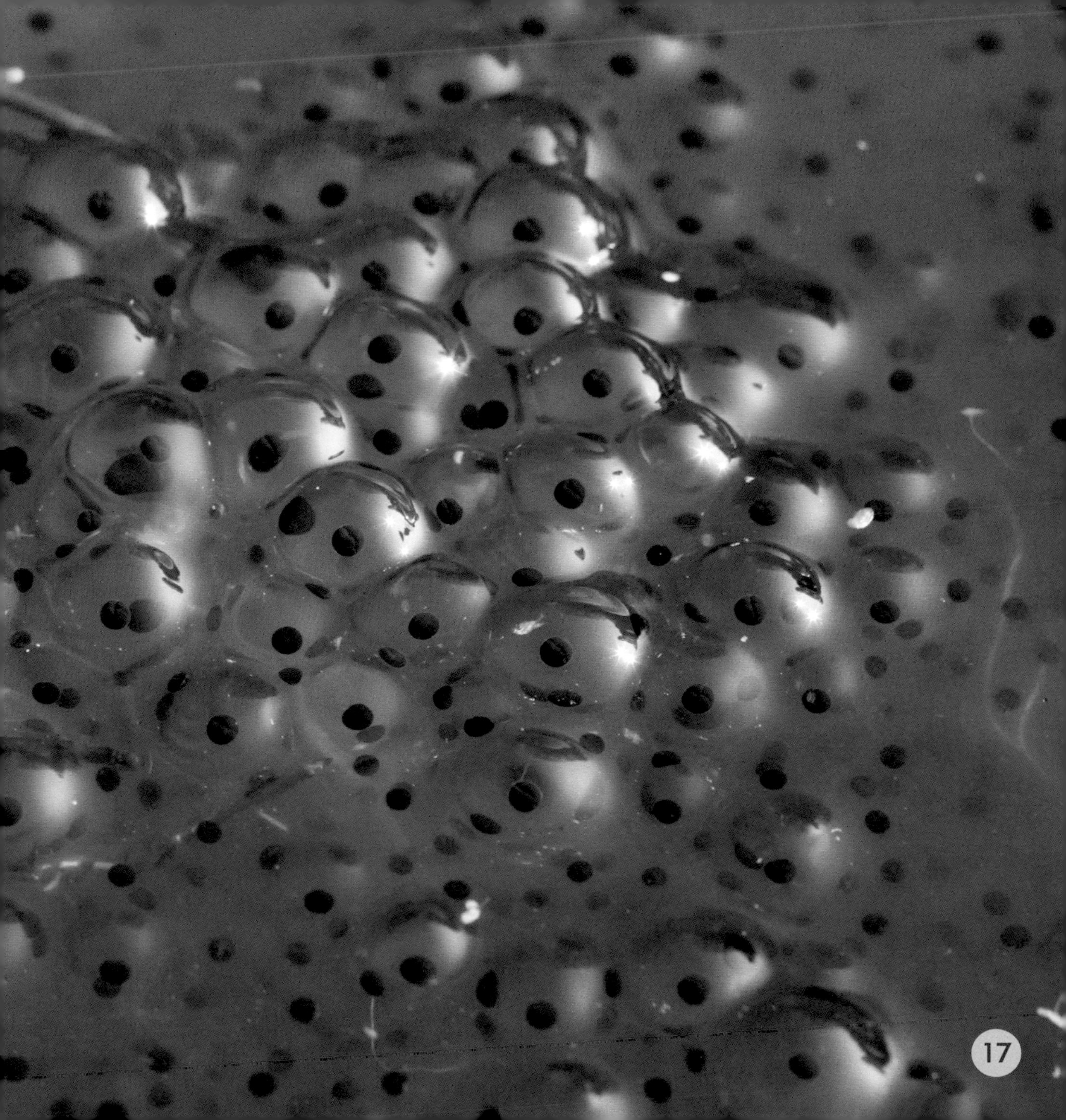

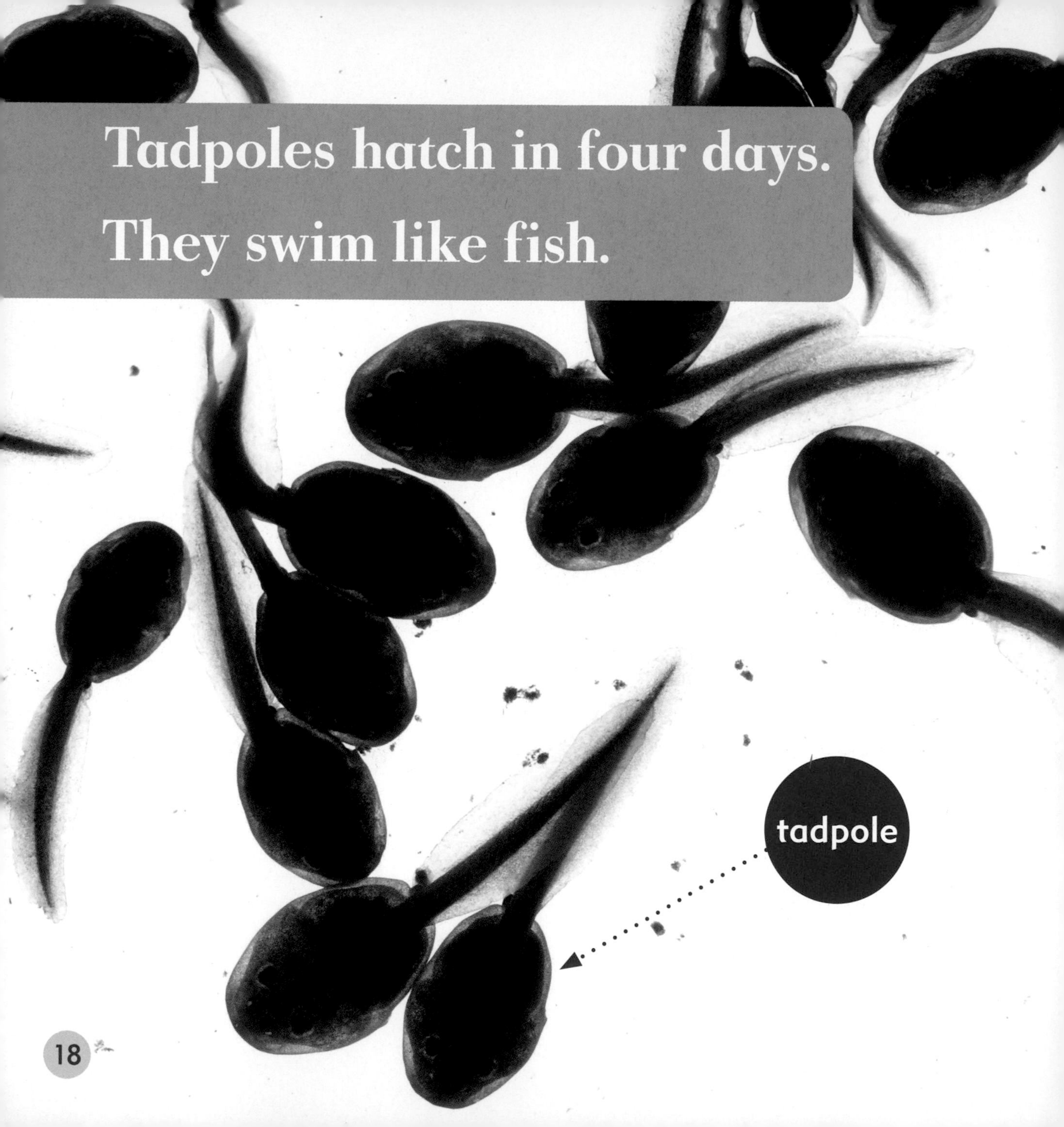

Tadpoles hatch in four days.
They swim like fish.

After a year, they grow legs.

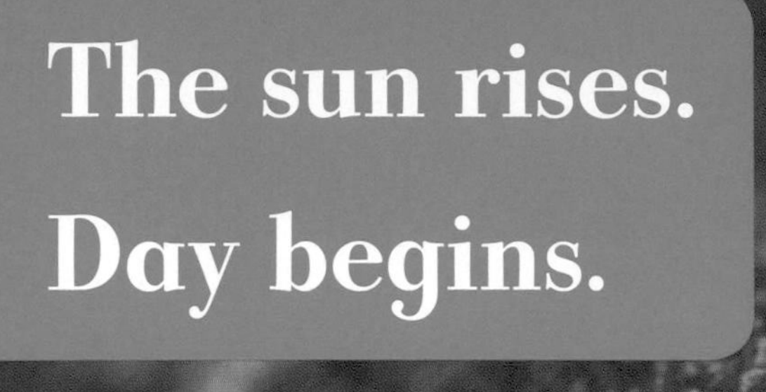

The sun rises.
Day begins.

Bullfrogs rest.

Parts of a Bullfrog

eyes
Bullfrog eyes peek out of the water.

mouth
Bullfrogs swallow prey with their big mouth.

legs
Long legs help bullfrogs leap.

webbed feet
Webbed feet help bullfrogs swim.

Picture Glossary

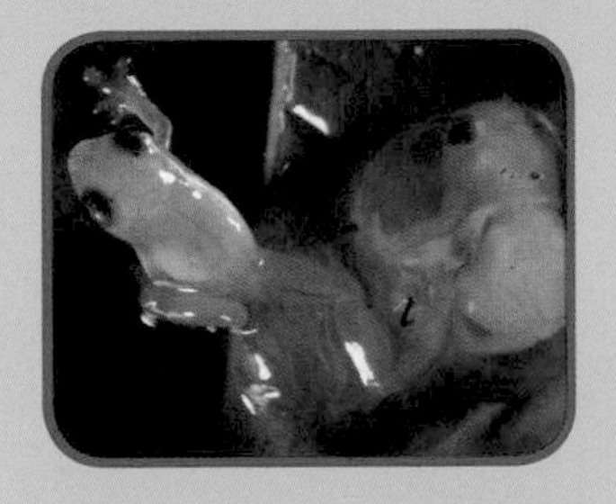

hatch
To break out of an egg.

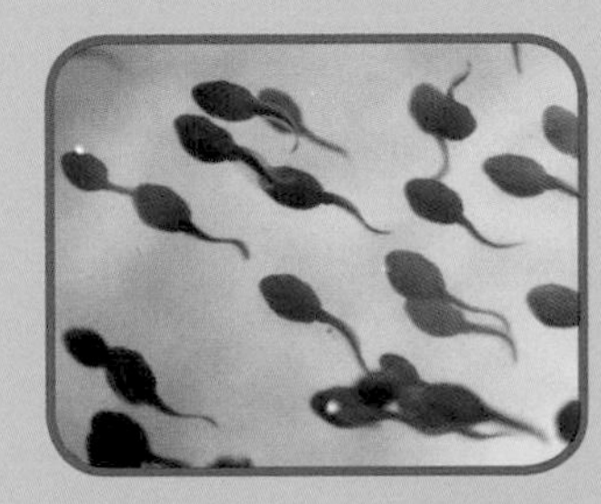

tadpole
A young frog.

leap
To jump up high over something.

webbed
Having skin between the toes.

Index

To Learn More

Learning more is as easy as 1, 2, 3.

1) Go to www.factsurfer.com

2) Enter "bullfrog" into the search box.

3) Click the "Surf" button to see a list of websites.

With factsurfer.com, finding more information is just a click away.

4/9/15